Over

JANE DRAYCOTT was born in London College London and Bristol University *Prince Rupert's Drop* (Carcanet/Oxford Forward Prize for Best Collection in 1999. In 2002 she was the winner of the Keats–Shelley Prize for Poetry and in 2004, the year of her second Carcanet/OxfordPoets collection, *The Night Tree*, she was nominated as one of the Poetry Book Society's 'Next Generation' poets. Her other books include *Christina the Astonishing* (with Lesley Saunders and Peter Hay, 1998) and *Tideway* (illustrated by Peter Hay, 2002), both from Two Rivers Press. She lives and works in Oxfordshire.

JANE DRAYCOTT

Over

Oxford*Poets*

CARCANET

First published in Great Britain in 2009 by
Carcanet Press Limited
Alliance House
Cross Street
Manchester M2 7AQ

A CIP catalogue record for this book is available from the British Library
ISBN 978 1 903039 92 2

The publisher acknowledges financial assistance from Arts Council England

Typeset by XL Publishing Services, Tiverton
Printed and bound in England by SRP Ltd, Exeter

For Norman

Acknowledgements

Thanks are due to the editors of the following publications in which some of these poems first appeared: *Atlas, Charms Against Jackals* (Two Rivers Press, 2004), *Divers* (Aark Arts, 2008), *Hand Luggage Only* (Open Poetry, 2007), *Horizon Review, Magma, Modern Poetry in Translation, Oranges and Sardines, Oxford Magazine, Oxford Poetry, Painted, spoken, Poetry London, Poetry Review, The Rialto, Times Literary Supplement*, www.blinking-eye.co.uk.

'We would like you to listen' and 'Concourse' are part of an audio-text collaboration with Elizabeth James based on the *Emblematum liber* of Andrea Alciato, 1531. 'Island' and 'The Funeral of Queen Victoria' were commissioned as part of the British Film Institute's 'Essentially British' Mediatheque project 2007; 'The Girls' Book of Model-Making' is indebted to fellow participants at Jo Shapcott's Henley Literary Festival 2007 workshop; 'The Hired Boat' was commissioned by Henley Literary Festival 2007; the extract from *Pearl* is from a new translation forthcoming from Carcanet Press, supported by Arts Council England, South East.

The closing words of 'Ashburnham House' are from Chris McCully's translation of the final part of *Beowulf* (*Old English Poems and Riddles*, Carcanet, 2008). 'Concourse' contains references to W.J.T. Mitchell, Susan Stewart and Anthony Vidler's *Antony Gormley: Blind Light* (Hayward Gallery Publishing, 2007). The line from Federico García Lorca's 'Romance Sonámbulo' in 'Mike' is from *Romancero gitano* (1928). Extracts from the song 'Baby, It's Cold Outside' in 'Foxtrot' are from Frank Loesser's original 1944 lyrics.

With thanks to Two Rivers Press and Jill Hay for making Peter Hay's linocut 'The Fig Tree' available, to Christopher and Marisa North for their hospitality at Almàssera Vella, and especially to fellow poets at the Poetry Workshop (founded 1983: see www.leonacarpenter.co.uk/wordpress) for their invaluable friendship and advice.

Contents

Over

Sky man

Waits at the wilderness
edge of your leaf eye.
Cloud mine. Your sky.
Palm fringed. Your eye.
Not you. You.

Waits at the stone gated
head of your river bed.
Fever of drapery.
Napalm of drapery.
Not you. You.

Waits in the ceiling fan
over the forest. Iris,
arena or snake-pit.
Last exit to naked.
Not you. You.

Waits in the sky mine
upriver. You are stone
and that chair is only a chair.
No change in the face of the mirror.
Not you. You.

The Square

Across the square a woman is looking at me
from a window, the shadow of the room she's in
pressing her like a flower towards the light.

In her sleeveless linen dress she is beautiful,
a cool candle in the vast dark glass,
like my mother in a time before I knew her.

Between us, a river of tourists, faces lifted
to the great bronze horses stepping off
into some other air we cannot see.

Like a lover across a room I return her look
but she in her eyes is saying *It's too late now*
and it is: I might as well be invisible.

Even if I crossed the square and found
that room she's in, she would be gone for sure.
She isn't interested in me any more.

In the pages of the outdated annual she found it, the bird
with terracotta wings. Like the little fish
beside it, it knew nothing of trouble and its hellish
landscape, its weight on the scales like some absurdly
growing thing.
                The bird seemed perfect, submerged
for ever in the womb that was the best
idea of bird: fields, canals and schist
seen from the air, and trouble barely heard.

Girls then wore their hair in shining helmets
and their brothers rushed across the lawn to swim
out from the shadows, from the stifling willows
between the wars.
                But now the world seemed different,
the birds, the fish, the sorrow. One hundred and one things
to make of it and all she feared might follow.

In the same way

In the same way, a man might leave a house
at dawn, closing the door as quietly as he can
(though still it echoes in the street like pack ice
or the trigger of a gun) and launch himself
across the local street-map on his bike.

He rides all day and night, he rides for years,
the stony tracks, the hills, the deep crevasses
and the bright blue light. Until one evening
like a total stranger on a pitch black road
the land puts up a hand and draws its knife.

So when he does return it's with a deep map
of the landscape carved into his face
as its catastrophes are locked into his voice.
All night the hills and crushing ice roll under him.
Sleep now, nobody can understand everything.

Pass

for Holly

We calculate you're two corners away by now,
first time alone in the car, navigating through
the twelve big houses at the edge of town,
the fallow field where once in a blue moon
a spring appears like a flying fish at sea.
The winter night's as clear as cooling glass
but you accelerate away from us too fast
to see the stars, the arrows on the ground.

Your music steers you on a sail of sound,
you are on fire. Your hands are Mercury,
your heart and eyes the Sun. You plough
the top road like a submarine – we try in vain
to visualise your course, the unlit shipping lanes,
the shoals of stars. We cannot see you now.

We would like you to listen

We would like you to listen
      with your whole body
that dog   Jimmy   circling
surprised by the moon   the mirror

To do so we would ask you to reflect
    that dog   is just calling   dog

We want to ask   what we can
    seeing himself   as others see him
another dog   we can   ultimately listen to

Jimmy   the point of living   is just to call
    is to merge   with the Beloved
to call   another dog

Longing or love   the moon's
    just rocks   another sea
circling there   surprised

Concourse

Selective walking in a field or maze.
Closed circuitry. Wave after wave
of closeness. Running together.

A deployment of human figures.
Seed bed. Our bed. We float,
are carried. You against me.

Now what? Get in close
with personal data. Me against you.
What are you going to do about it?

Get in close. *You made this world.*

The Longest Day

i.m. NPD

The stonework's vault from the pull of the crypt
   in the tallest cathedral in Europe,
the topmost stone in the bridge's fan,
    the waist of a diamond, a sea-eagle's span

or you at fifteen, poised on the high board,
    arms toward heaven in what might be prayer
or praise to the sun and what you can dare
    before the slow-curving dive to the cold

at the foot of the cliff or pier, that day
    at the height of summer, exactly half-way.

Ashburnham House

*A Fire broke out in the House of Mr Bently, adjoining to
the King's School near Westminster Abbey*
Gentleman's Magazine, 1731

Within that mansion, many men sleeping.
Caught between darkness and dawn
they dream of a mansion, a hall
where all are safe and speak the language.

In the library, *Beowulf*, *Genesis*,
songs within songs and the start
of a flame sparked by something
still live in the hearth beyond curfew.

Then, monstrous illumination, an invasion
of gold like a heat-seeking missile tracing
a line through each manuscript blown
like a seafarers' beacon into the oil-dark air

from which arise voices, trapped
in the heat like speech in a sandstorm.
Wherefore look you so sadly? A woman's lament
at the pyre of her homeland: *Alas!*

Of the men who had dreamed of the mansion,
their night-shirts were sails. As fire begat fire
each Englishman watched from his small boat
out on the lawn. *Heaven swallowed the smoke.*

Turquoise

Because it is so necessary.

In the shop they are looking
for bits of sky. It is in his eyes.
She is in his eyes, sacred object,
talisman against some kind
of falling. Her eyes are turquoise,
tending towards fire. Like heaven.
Inlaid like heaven on earth.

And here it is, at least
a little bit of it. Blue fire.

★

At sea they watch the sky free falling,
a line of fire tending towards green,
towards the underwater mines of green.

And now they swim. Cold, deep, downward.
Because it is impossible. Now she is scared.

After the Meal

After the meal (for this is the hour) comes
      the helicopter. Each person's plate
wiped clean as an ice-field, miraculous flight

to rise like a mythical insect over the mountains,
      the legendary gardens hanging like hair,
then lower one's body and winch down the post.

This is the hour when husbands and wives
      at their tables gaze at each other amazed,
like looking at photos of earth from the air,

the miles of mangrove, its jewelled brocade,
      or their own letters found in their parents' effects
or the wonderful clothes they once wore.

This is the hour in the high alpine restaurants
      when lovers of many years' standing
wonder if they have ever existed at all.

All this was fields

All this was fields and the mental hospital
        lying under a guesswork of snow

She had the most beautiful eyes like green jewels
and a strange mouth dubious and dodgy
        next door they were adopted

When I think of the unmarried mothers' home
I think of snow and the long drive like a story
        you'll never know the ending of

It was all fields and something must have
        been planted there while we were away

Night Museum

for KP

It fills the window like a picture framed,
fine-printed feathers on a glass-walled cave,
an owl that took the solid pane for air,
astonished breast and wings a five-point star
like fire engraved in frost, a comrade caught
on camera at the instant of the shot.

The pre-dawn galleries are darkened fields
where objects yield their store of buried heat:
faint pencil markings in the great composer's
hand, a thought in flight, the poet-soldier's
notebook and his heart-stopped watch,
the lava casts, the legendary shroud –

almost the body, the thing itself outstretched
but with the life withdrawn, back into the woods.

The Fair Miles

It is with the utmost difficulty that we have observed Astraea
George Airy, Greenwich 1847

To and fro along the fair miles
the fascinations travel, coming in
along the cloud lined avenue
to his small astronomer's eye.
Under the ancient tree, its inky leaves,
he watches, chained to the hill
and sleepless. *When was last light?*
Distant winds, charmed lives.

He stares into the thickening shade,
its blossoming city-constellations,
runways, street lamps, flowerbeds.
Star lilies, honesty and thrift.
Each night he searches for her,
smaller than he remembers,
gazing up at him beside a tree
waiting in their first garden.

Mass Observation

Under his watch old woman
sixty-five with son and daughter
right-hand smoker just lets fag
touch lips does not inhale.

One of the group goes out
those left say *night* immortal
words a kind of chorus *night*
see thee in morning

gaze at the departing one
from knees to shoes at which
they stare as if they'd never
seen the like before.

Outside the two blue doors
three men late twenties
scan the dimmer constellations
sky exceptionally clear.

Quay Street

Only that it moved in ways with its haunches
among the gantries, that something like claw-marks
or fire had appeared at the door to the cold store,
that the aerial photos showed nothing.

That it came in on ships, that it moved
upon the waters in the manner of its homeland,
that its skin, that the gold of its eye, that it
could be heard singing. Not frightened exactly.

Island

Noon and the whole island quiet. Not one hammer
or saw to be heard from the silent interior, no voices
snagged on the wind, not even the mad. Is this illness?

Perhaps the answer lies in their adits and crypts
or in these gateposts and their monumental claim to space,
The Beauty of Melancholy carved out on their hills.

Then at last we see them, down on the shoreline
gazing out to sea without a word between them,
waiting for the new world and what it might bring.

Except for the boy at the very centre of the group,
hand on the coastguard's bell, looking directly at us.

Opera Express

Each night he worked, child paid to applaud:
the penniless young lovers, the soprano
who thought she would live for ever.
At home the furniture was burnt or sold.
Only his mother in her winter bed remained,
and him by day pushing his silent train
across the ice and continent of floor.

Each night they came from Brno, Prague,
the adults in their diamonds and furs.
The train arrived, it filled the stage
though no voice spoke or sang.
Each night he clapped his frozen hands
to break the silence, keep his body warm.
I heard him once, the tiny hands, the storm.

Eldorado

Forty days in an open boat
     drifting in the gas-green wilderness,
carnevale – farewell, farewell –
     the whole crew fighting to put
the beach back into the thermos
     (Balbec, Salcombe),
the ocean back into the woods
     where rocking gently you might
begin again, *berceuse*, hearts
     of oak, a house in the forest.

What lies ahead's impossible – dwindling
     provisions, the mud-choked delta.
From here ascend the Orinoco,
     rising again through shrieking trees
into Arcadia, the world turned
     upside down, Cockaigne,
which now begins to look a lot
     like home. There is no gold.

The Funeral of Queen Victoria

(The Procession Starting from Victoria Station)

This is the terminus where it all begins
like Speke at the source of the Nile,
this soot-laden palm-house where time
like a great iron seed will be kept
and stored *in memoriam*, bearing her name.

The streets are a sea-bed revealed
by a parting of souls for her gun-carriage
hauled on its voyage to darkness
like Cleopatra's Needle towed
to the sunless banks of the Thames.

What votive gifts go with her now?
Scale models of water pumps sent
to the East with her earnest good wishes,
commemorative clocks, the Bible
in ten different tongues and a copy

of Bradshaw's great Railway Guide
to the Underworld: which slow train
to take on the route over infinite sands
to face the colossal throne of Osiris,
encounter those gods at first hand.

Lookout Mountain

The vast reflectors, gears
and rings of brass to be carried up
on the backs of mules.

One man to open a lantern
and shine it across the ravine
to another man waiting. *Send, send.*

To call and to wait.
Smoke and haze to rise
from the ancient forest floor.

Using the mirrors, the speed
of the answering light to be measured.
Your younger self shimmering.

All that we have

for Lil

All that we have   the great arch
with the floors fallen away   and high
above tree-level   a fireplace breasting the sky

Below like the plate   you dropped on the hearth
that Christmas Day   an overgrown knot-garden
family book-plate   holding its pattern

the code to the universe   the rug in the hall
the sweet-smelling pathways   not ruined at all

from *Pearl*

One thing I know for certain: that she
was peerless, pearl who would have added
light to any prince's life
however bright with gold. None
could touch the way she shone
in any light, so smooth, so small,
she was a jewel above all others.
So pity me the day I lost her
in this garden where she fell
beneath the grass into the earth.
I stand bereft, struck to the heart
with love and loss. My spotless pearl.

I've gazed a hundred times at the place
she left me, grieving for that gift
which swept away all shadow, that face
which was the antidote to sorrow.
Although this watching sears my heart
and wrings the wires of sadness tighter,
the song this silence sings to me
is the sweetest I have heard:
the countless quiet hours in which
her pale face floats before me, mired
in mud and soil, a perfect jewel
spoiled, my spotless pearl.

In the place where such riches lie rotting
a carpet of spices will surely spread,
blossoms of blue and white and red
which fire in the full light facing the sun.
Where a pearl is planted deep in the dark
no fruit or flower could ever fade;
all grasscorn grows from dying grain
so new wheat can be carried home.
From goodness other goodness grows:
so beautiful a seed can't fail
to fruit, or spices fail to flower
fed by such a spotless pearl.

So I came to this very same spot
in the green of an August garden, height
and heart of the summer, at Lammas time
when corn is cut with curving scythes.
And I saw that the little hill where she fell
was a shaded place showered with spices:
pink gillyflower, ginger and purple gromwell
powdered with peonies scattered like stars.
But more than their loveliness to the eye,
the sweetest fragrance seemed to float
in the air there also. I knew beyond doubt
that's where she lay. My spotless pearl.

Caught in grief's chill grasp I stood
in that place and clasped my hands, seized
by the grip on my heart of longing and loss.
Though reason told me to be still,
I mourned for my poor imprisoned pearl
with all the fury and force of a quarrel.
The comfort of Christ called out to me,
but still I wrestled in wilful sorrow.
The power and perfume of those flowers
filled up my head and felled me, slipped me
into sudden sleep in that place
where she lay beneath me. My girl.

Return to Relleu

for Sophie

It has taken us two hours to walk back
from Maria's bar, the best paella in the region
weighing inside me like a baby.

Among these olive groves, these tiers
of hills, we might have been climbing up
through Palestine or Ancient Greece.

We come down now in darkness, Orion
and the Pleiades. The church has turned to gold,
the oranges are constellations in their trees.

For a moment I believe I can see beech woods,
bluebells, and you there in the window seat
waiting, looking outward to a distant sea.

In your lap, *The World's Great Myths*.
Reading and waiting, although not for me,
for someone in another time than this.

Picnic

We are lying very close to the ground
as if we'd thrown ourselves down
           at the approach of enemy aircraft

or because in a gale it's the one thing
that won't be blown to pieces like everything else.

You've opened the bottle and are offering me choice facts
laid out like a cold beef salad:
           the twelve richest men in Britain,

the five different voices on your car navigation system,
the total time in hours we've been together.

What you don't know is that there's a low fuse of fire
and coming storm snaking its way
           through the long grass towards us.

It has lain a little way off just stirring quietly in snow
and sunlight among the beech-mast all these years

though you've never been able to hear it, nailed down
to the past as you are like an old carpet.
           When it hits, you are telling me again

about the amazing young man who only ever
painted from memory, perfect in every detail.

Technique

A house is a good large object to visualise
'Seeing With the Mind's Eye', Samuels & Samuels

Walk slowly round it, then picture yourself
in one of the rooms. Now move through
the rest of the house as if you were a camera.
The kitchen's a back street in a labyrinth
of slums, impossibly hot, where the heroine's
hopelessly lost but daren't stop searching
though her kids both sense something's
terribly wrong. In the back room a woman
sits on the stoop with her head on her knees
since a tornado's wrecked every inch
of the cabin she had held together for years.
Now visualise the hallway (something like
a Hitchcock, one jacket on the coat-stand,
the key swinging in the door as if possessed),
then up to the landing where two children, girls,
are struggling in a plunging torrent to save the dog
and precious childhood toys caught in the flood.
Finally go back to the room you first visualised,
the one with the mirror, then look outside
at the men circling the house, the one just leaving.

Door

Everything must go in through the one door:
horses, carriages (which disintegrate early
after installation), armour, jewels, seeds.

Larger objects such as cliff-tops, lakes
and public squares are atomised and labelled
for reconstruction piece by piece.

The effect is startling, like a kind
of bolt-hole. Timeless. Even the chock
of footsteps and the movement of the stars.

All it takes is a peasant working in a field
to make the initial find – an ancient buckle
or a new-born baby in amongst the wheat.

Wayzgoose

Waist-high the wheat is talking, the great
conversation. We motor past, foreheads
to the glass, and climb through hedgerow
margins to the edge of the known world.

On the hill's broad back, offered like snow
without a sound, we now lay out
the argument and patterning of our feast.

Where we have come, summer applies
its even weight to tarmac, cornfields
and the silent lake where no ink lies.

Where we are going, the goose has
in her eye and takes her onward flight,
nib-neck leading toward the season
of quiet work by candlelight.

Wayzgoose: an annual excursion for printing employees,
traditionally 24 August (St Bartholomew's Eve).

The Hired Boat

They wanted a boat that would ferry them upstream
away from the chaos of sea, a boat
named *Shalott* or *Narcissus* which rowed like a dream
while they took it in turns to tell stories or spoke
in brief fragments that surfaced then sank in the mud.

They rowed into darkness, its wingspan or rib-cage
of hills, up the glassy spine of the valley,
each stroke like a heartbeat or turn of a page.
By morning they'd vanished, their boat in the shallows
no more than a leaf or the eye of a bird

which drank at the glittering throat of the flood
where it narrowed to only a single word.

Over

Alpha

End of summer in the apartments.
On their rope-walks across the city
the dry months tauten to quiet.

At night, the ear gondolas through
the narrow echoing hours, the heart
slap-slapping under bridges
of sometimes only a single word.

Through the caverns of brickwork
we listen for vital signs – the man
below echo-finding on his radio,
a piano trickling with water,

winter with its chloroform mornings
pulsing hundreds of miles offshore:
begin, begin, begin.

Bravo

i.m. JP

Down the middle of our street's a table
where odds and evens might meet
and its cloth is the skirt of the night-duty nurse
or an altar prepared for a feast.

It's midnight but it's not that scary
when you've been in the woods
as often as we have, and it's tranquil.

This is not the darkness you think it is –
see how vision deepens: dashboard dials,
rain on a kerbstone, the blurred heart
of a bird in flight, icebergs everywhere.

On the night-table, sugar in infinite detail,
sweetmeats, silver in the shape of a prayer,
something from every house in the road.

Fear nothing. It is not over yet.
Soon we will have a whole city of light.

Charlie

Now here you are at the airport
speaking five different languages at least
with ease, five unbelievable necklaces

one of which might just be
the song of a blackbird
as you precision-skate the runway,

conquistador three days without sleep,
to now take flight, carrying
everything you know up the mountain.

Above the snowline even your hair sings.
You turn again to almost perfect crystal,
you are beyond the shadow of a doubt.

And from the peak you see it, one glimpse
before it's smothered by a cloud-filled sky.
Bye-bye blackbird, bye-bye.

Delta

And so your hard-won boat
      ends up here, disintegrating
    after the long trip down

toward these seven channels of light,
      high summer fanning out ahead:
    papyrus, lily flowers, their bell-mouthed *ah*.

You have become a house with corridors
      open to the sky, your triangular heart
    a sail or garden, fertile ground

for those you know to come
      and live in, in a sort of reverie
    before you break up altogether,

drift out into international waters,
      not recoverable now.

Echo

While you wait
    the phoney war

Lightning and thunder
    signal and action

Something and nothing
    force and reaction

Over over
    eye of the hurricane

Déjà déjà vu

Foxtrot

i.m. PBD

Baby it's cold outside – that was you
singing out just now, giving me
your straight look from the dusk
of wherever you are now dancing
in your red silk dress with Daddy.

I'll hold your hands, they're just like ice.
You have seen something terrifying
in the alley at the bottom of the garden
and cry, then swift are gone again
chasing the small birds and voles.

I cannot imagine what it is like
out there in the wild, foraging for scraps
(*look out the window at that storm*)
but I say dry your eyes now: *in the cool
cool cool of the evening, let's put out the lights.*

Darling Lily – your cry sparks out again
across the neighbourhood and then
you are gone and all the things you are
headed out for open country.
Darling Lily. C'est magnifique.

Golf

In the mirage we saw three figures, kings
perhaps or the type with the migrant gene –
adventurous, always one step ahead

striking a path through the desert simply
by instinct, first to smell the oasis,
first then to gaze on the moon in the well.

We struck out towards them. It felt as if
boundless and bare the morning might take us
and carry us elsewhere, somewhere ahead

which wasn't a carpet of dandelions
struck by the clock of the wind again and again
and no one to blame but yourself.

Between us and the men who looked like us
a river, an ocean of sand, a gulf.

Hotel

*In the last days, the only place you could be sure of lunch
was the Imperial Hotel*

Harp was news from elsewhere gathering
in scales across the ornamental lake,
the small pond and the swimming pool.

Heart was hers gazing with all the patience
of fishermen and their silence downwards
past the sharpening tongues of water

and in through *Casement* which was green glass
opening in the water's deeper wall,
valve into some older river's road.

Carp was a silent order, mysterious domain,
a golden age stored in a dark barn,
water expanding in a previous summer's heat.

Paper was a small red salmon curling
in her palm, the open offer of a feast,
a future known, fish always on Fridays.

India

At the gates
of the fabulous
city of gold

out of the blue
he told her
the truth

and the whole world
tipped, was dipped
in sudden indigo

like a late-running messenger
or working beyond dark
in the fields.

Juliet

She's leaving   leaving
the oak-panelled bar at the Hôtel des Rêves
        walking right out
through the trees   and the thorn-bushes
        putting behind her   the spindles of sleep.

She's leaving   pushing her way
        through the roulette wheel
of the five-pointed door   stepping out
like the wife in the weather house
            just as he enters.

She's crossing the road   to the beach
        where the sea air's implying
more darkness   the ocean is black
    with things unforeseen
and the starfish lie pale and inert.

It's midnight.   She enters the water
    the forest of sharp-bladed coral
the fruit   which is not what it seems.
It's midnight   she's leaving
        she's leaving   the Hotel of Dreams.

Kilo

In that short space — the marsh ice parting,
rising to flood and shrinking again to thistles
as thirty-odd years sank like an archipelago
behind him — the reed-carrier's story was told.

Untold, the very good reason he left his boat,
crossed by the weir or meadow in hours of darkness
or daylight, walked downstream to the city of gold
or up to the silent gardens of the nunnery

his boat pre-dating all accurate maps, his voice
in the reeds inaudible even to our long ears,
his load taking up only so much draught
in the telling, so much weight on our page.

Lima

In Europe the interior has become a genre
in its own right, light from outside streaming
like silver in through the windows of merchants,
the whole world held like linen before the press.

At the workshops the telescope's perfected
(*a device to allow one to see one's
enemies or count coins from a long way off*),
the ships, the idols, the distant city of mist.

In the lens-grinder's glass they are all one.
The map-maker's work is also complete,
El Teatro del Todo el Mundo: the mountains,
the scourges, the large crowds out on the streets.

Mike

Remove the sandals from your feet, for the place where you stand is holy

Joshua 5:15

Surgeon, maybe clockmaker: as a child
they'd marvelled at his touch with butterflies
and woodlice, as if he loved the world,
its bones and feathers, better than himself.

In the diary they found photos. Him splitting
the rock with lightning, standing like a minder
on mountain tops, a paratrooper fully armed –
the sword, the secret name, the word of God.

There too his sketches for the wings:
viridian hummingbird, the mallard's sheen,
a lawn in June, the perilous emerald sea.

Verde que te quiero verde. The book of life,
the earth. His hands which never trembled.
His burning hours. *It isn't about me.*

November

Demonstrating the art of silent killing
(from handshake to fatal collapse in a matter
of seconds) her sleeve trembles, she wishes
the naked mountains clothed in leaves.

There is nothing she can't teach them
about life in the field: surveillance, nights
up to the shins in an ice-bearing tide,
the frost-hardened heart, the use of the knife.

Worst of all is severance of contact
with those you love most, the land as green
as a jewel one minute then pulled like a carpet
of daisies or violets from under your feet.

Avoid carrying parcels, don't hang about.
Commit nothing to paper, memorise
if you can – the face of a daughter, eye-colour,
hair, the lilies she dropped as she ran.

When challenged by strangers pretend
to have forgotten everything: *aren't those*
flowers over there? Success is to pass
unrecognised by even your closest friends.

Oscar

*The marriage of Prince Oscar of Sweden to Miss Ebba Munck took place
quietly on Thursday at Bournemouth*

New York Times, March 1888

To the secrets of the pleasure grounds
               and of the painted panorama
To the imitation marble staircase
               and the slightly damp sheets
To marriage, its veil of snow
               like dust on a piano
To the performance by the town of itself
               including the esplanades daily
To the Winter Gardens,
               their surprising heat
To the sea-fog
               the arms of its mist
Yes they said, *Yes.*

Papa

The talk was of how he'd set out in the spring
once the ice had cleared and his terror of snow
receded into its cave, how he'd spear
the winter months and cure them, save
the best of the apples, prepare good lengths
of rope to keep him safe whatever happened
then sit and speak with us about his deep
love of the sea.
                        And indeed light had just
begun to fill the room and a faint white quality
of air to rise like a thin glass dome
over the town (though to us the ice
seemed solid still as stone) the day he came down
and taking with him nothing set out alone.

Quebec

Last night you called across the ice-pillow,
the question you'd been carving all winter.
Snow knife, air knife, the children deep in sleep.

Too chill for instruments, you sang: throat wreath
for a stilled land – rivers frozen like words
on the tongue, the vast bay, the terrifying cold.

So in this séance-season we each mourn,
nights back to back with night, or else turn,
the body closest on this silent plain

and lip to lip breathe winter's only answer –
the solitary owl in the darkness,
the beauty of the ice-journey, its flame.

Romeo

He was the gardener. He had turned the orchard of fruitless trees into an oasis of green and gold, and was at work trimming the vines when he saw her. She stood in the shade of the pomegranate tree, a small glass in her hand like a rose-coloured jewel.

It was Easter. In the square they were preparing to bring down the body of Christ and carry the Mother of God on a palanquin right through the streets, rocking with grief. After that day, nothing could keep them apart. When she prayed she asked to die before he did.

Sierra

I have traced the route one final time with my finger, the veins of
streams, the cliffs and hollows. I can see it as if we'd walked it
already: the wind-shaved stone at the pass where we shall eat our
rations, the cairn, the evening where the rock gives way to grass.
This mist unsettles and delays us. I have divided up the chocolate
you gave me so it will last – by Easter Monday I shall be home and
all the chocolate finished. Last night the rain ran in a narrow stream
through the tent, a path from which it could not be diverted.

Tango

We in the south of the city
had taken the glass from our windows,
cleared the rail-yards and roads
for his coming velocity.

Strict and dry he amazed us
with his textbook footwork,
explosions of movement and pauses
in orange, concrete and red.

Down on the estuary tearing up
steamers and ferries he danced like one
who had taken leave of this world.

So he has left us in this new dark age,
listening at the gatepost for the next
coming style, looking at the sky.

Uniform

She wore them whenever she left
the house, the tear-drop earrings,
scarab watch and timeless solitaire.

She wore them whenever she felt afraid
and never thought of them as fallen
bits of stars or like the tears of God

but got down on her hands and knees
and kissed the ground to see
just how much light a stone,
a solid piece of earth cut right, could yield.

She wore them then especially at night
and saw how schooled in darkness
they had learned to catch the light
and keep it, adamantine, adamant.

Victor

What took our breath away was how
in our fox-red coats and marble skin
we more than filled the streets, the village
a toy-town under our ten-league boots,
the sky still married to the small pond,
the stream still headed for somewhere else.

What we'd imagined was a cathedral
in which we'd weigh nothing. But here
in the marketplace we stand alert
and larger even than in life,
night vision tracking for the far end
of the alley and open country.

Whiskey

A match struck
in the house of ice.

Deep-sea flame fish
calling, the heart

harpooning. Something
in the dark is flashing.

Gold in the blood,
everything you know.

The fire on the little sandy beach.
The bear at the window.

No one escapes.

X-ray

Sky Harbor International Airport will test a new federal screening system
that takes X-rays of passengers' bodies

USA Today, December 2006

It is late. At the gates to her city
she calls your name, yes you, moon moth
pinned here on the pages of this open book.
So much yourself and not like you at all.

The night is carbon. You are long past sleep.
Here at the crossing point you meet
her scanning eye in silence, though
there's much more you could tell.

How you played the violin each night
at gunpoint, how you sang among the dead
in Thrace, how you come as a messenger,
bring news from another place.

Yankee

In the forty-acre cornfield
    where every stalk is cut
by gunfire to the ground
    as closely as a knife.
In the burned-out apricot groves
    and in the locust tree
slashed down in the yard.
    At Sunken Road and Babylon,
Da Nang and Mossy Creek.
    And in the diary, his last entry,
By this river I was killed.
    Among the horses loose in the woods.

Zulu

One thing my father never did
was slip out under the mimosa trees
at dawn to where the blacksmith
in the last patches of night was already
at work on the *iklwa* blade, beautiful
as a new leaf, a young fish hurtling,
named for the sound it would make
in and out of the body – *iklwa*.
Nor as a boy single-handedly kill
a leopard down from the plump hills –
mountain saffron, iron-wood, assegai –
nor to his clan (named for the heavens
or sky) bring great victory or pride
though working late on summer evenings
amongst the trees of our small orchard
he did make us a playground out of oak
and ropes and hammering well beyond dark,
a nail for every port he'd ever sailed to,
and then come in and play for hours
on our old Broadwood, his fingers
truly a river in spate around the house
and out into the desert of our street,
named for the small hill on which we lived.

Selected titles from the Oxford*Poets* list

Oxford*Poets*, an imprint of Carcanet Press, celebrates the vitality and diversity of contemporary poetry in English.

Joseph Brodsky *Collected Poems in English*
For Brodsky, to be a poet was an absolute, a total necessity...scintillating deployment of language, and always tangential or odd ways of interpreting ideas, events or other literature. John Kinsella, OBSERVER

Greg Delanty *Collected Poems 1986–2006*
A body of work that has grown steadily from book to book in depth, invention, and ambition. AGENDA

Jane Draycott *The Night Tree*
Hers is a scrupulous intelligence...Her searching curiosity and wonderful assurance make her an impeccable and central poetic intelligence. Penelope Shuttle, MANHATTAN REVIEW

Sasha Dugdale *The Estate*
Dugdale creates a spare, mythical tone that fits itself perfectly to the elemental Russian landscape in which much of her collection is set. GUARDIAN

Rebecca Elson *A Responsibility to Awe*
This is a wise and haunting volume, which I can't recommend too warmly. Boyd Tonkin, INDEPENDENT

Marilyn Hacker *Essays on Departure*
Everything is thrilling and true, fast and witty, deep and wise; her vitality is the pulse of life itself. Derek Mahon

Peter Scupham *Collected Poems*
The sophistication of the technique which underpins every poem becomes clearer and clearer as you read further in this substantial, generous, distinguished volume. Peter Davidson, Books of the Year 2005, READYSTEADYBOOK.COM

Charles Tomlinson *Cracks in the Universe*
Tomlinson is a unique voice in contemporary English poetry, and has been a satellite of excellence for the past 50 years. David Morley, GUARDIAN

Marina Tsvetaeva *Selected Poems*, trans. Elaine Feinstein
Feinstein has performed the first, indispensable task of a great translator: she has captured a voice. THREEPENNY REVIEW

Chris Wallace-Crabbe *By and Large*
His allies are words, and he sues them with the care of a surgeon and the flair of a conjuror. Peter Porter